Table Saw Handbook For Beginners

Complete Guide To Use Table Saw And Cut Angles

Copyright@2023

Eason Merrick

Table of content

CHAPTER ONE

Instructional guide Use Table Saw

A table saw is an adaptable piece of machinery that is simple to use and has the potential to save you both time and effort. Cutting boards requires the use of table saws, which are capable of making either large vertical cuts known as rips or shorter angled cuts known as crosscuts. You are able to create cuts that are exact and precise when you use your table saw if you adhere to the required procedures, have the appropriate safety equipment, and correctly set up your saw.

Section 1-Keeping Yourself Safe

1-When operating the table saw, always be sure to protect both your eyes and ears.

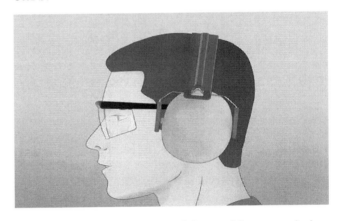

When cutting boards with a table saw, it is important to protect your eyes by using safety goggles or a hardhat with a visor. Sawdust and other debris from the wood will not be able to fly into your face or eyes if you do this. In addition, appropriate ear protection should be worn since saw blades may produce a very loud noise that can damage one's eardrums. For the purpose of protecting your hearing, you may buy earplugs that are either inexpensive and disposable or earmuffs that are more robust.

2-When cutting boards that are not very thick, you should use either a push shoe, a push stick, or a splitter.

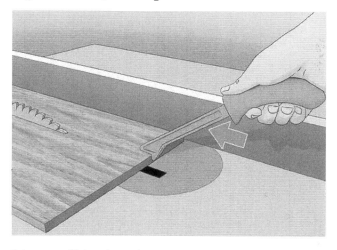

It's possible that there won't be much room for your hands between the blade and the side fence while you're cutting boards that are narrow and short. Because of this, you should make use of a push stick or a sled with notches in it to assist in guiding the wood while it is being cut. These table saw pushing devices are available for purchase at hardware shops and online. Alternatively, you may make your own or construct them yourself.

● Some push devices will contain elements that are adjustable so that they can accommodate various dimensions of wood.

3-Make use of clearance inserts.

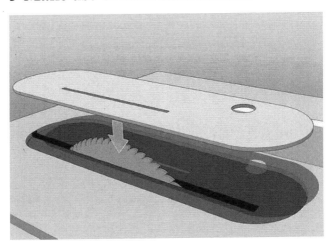

When you are ripping extremely thin boards, you should use an insert so that your fingers are not so near to the blade. This will keep them safer. When cutting very thin pieces of wood, it is helpful to have a buffer zone between the saw blade and the side fence. An insert is a piece of wood that may be inserted into this space.

● When cutting very thin boards, in addition to using the use of a clearing insert, you need also make use of a pushing device.

4-Make sure the blade guard is installed correctly.

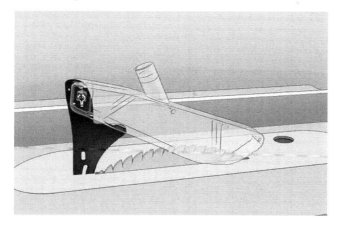

Protecting your fingers and preventing debris from kicking back are the two primary purposes that blade guards serve. If the blade guard is not already installed, you may either buy a new one from the manufacturer of your table saw or reinstall the one that was included with the table saw when it was first purchased. It is possible to reattach many contemporary blade guards to your blade by simply placing the guard on top of the blade and securing it with screws or plastic clamps.

5-Do not cut boards that have become twisted.

Boards that have been warped or twisted will produce harsh cuts, which will cause the wood to kick back. Do not make use of any boards that have warped or been damaged by water in any way.

6-Find the button that turns off the emergency power supply.

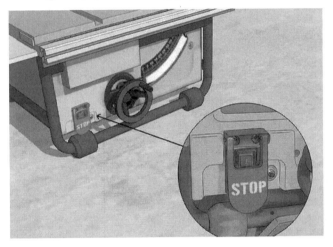

The majority of table saws are equipped with a sizable button or paddle that may be used as an emergency stop. It is possible that you may need to immediately switch off your machine in the event of an accident or if a board is kicking back. This button may be pressed with your leg quite a few times if your hands are otherwise busy.

7-Stay away from clothes and jewelry that hangs loosely about your body.

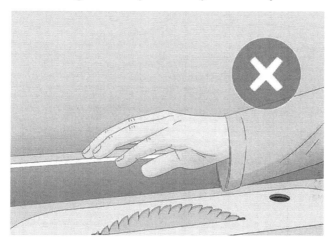

It is important to remember not to wear anything that might get caught in the saw, such as loose sleeves or a tie. Other items of clothes that are too baggy or loose fitting might get caught in the saw and drag you closer to it. If you have long hair, you should pull it back and secure it before using the table saw.

8-Make sure you read the instruction manual handbook first.

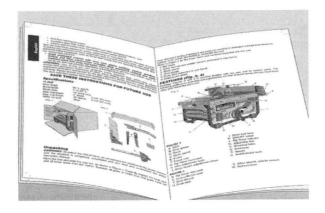

Be careful to give the instructions that came with your saw a thorough read before attempting to use it correctly or install it. Although most table saws are comparable to one another, there are notable distinctions between brands. By reading the handbook, you will get familiar with the location of each component of the saw, as well as its function and the appropriate measures of care that should be taken while using your particular model.

Section 2-Cutting Boards (Ripping Boards)

1-Raise the height of the blade till it is more than the thickness of the wood you are working with.

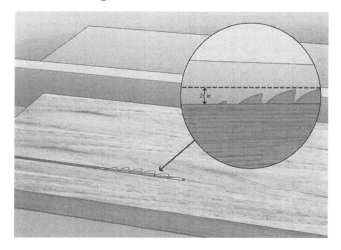

It is important to ensure that the blades of the saw are as thick as the thickness of the wood piece that you are cutting in order to prevent any possible backlash from occurring. To change the height of the blade on your table saw, locate the handle that is labeled "blade adjustment" and turn it counterclockwise. The height of the blade should be adjusted so that it is about a quarter of an inch (0.635 cm) higher than the thickness of the wood that you plan to cut.

2-Adjust the width of the fence that has to be cut to fit your dimensions.

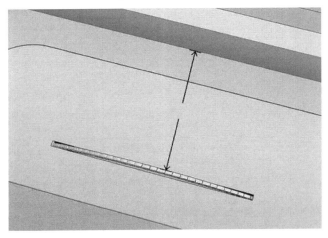

To determine the distance between the saw blade and the fence, measure it using a tape measure. You will have a handle at your disposal that, depending on how you turn it, will either tighten or loosen the side rail,

allowing you to move it from left to right.
You will need to move the side fence to the
appropriate distance before you can cut
your board.

- You would measure a distance of 2 feet
  (61 cm) between the side fence and the
  saw blade, for instance, if you needed
  to cut a board that was 2 feet (61 cm)
  broad.

**3-Lean the wood up against the fence in
this position.**

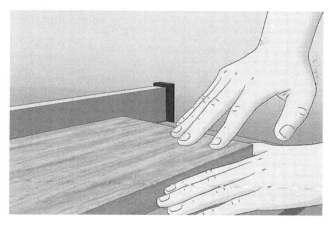

Put your thumb and hand behind the piece
of wood that is positioned between the

fence and the saw blade, and do it with caution. In order to stop the wood from kicking back, secure it securely against the table saw and the side fence.

4-Remove the blade guard and start the table saw after lowering it.

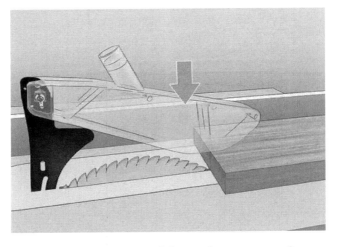

Put yourself in a position of greater safety by lowering the plastic guard blade over the blade. Prepare to cut by turning on the blade of the cutting tool.

5-Move your board such that it passes through the blade.

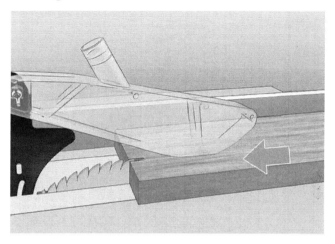

Move your board through the blade at a pace that is both slow and consistent. As you work to drive the board through, be sure to maintain its alignment with the fence at all times. You should never place your hand near the blade, and you should always use a push device or an insert if there is less than 6 inches (15.24 cm) of space between your hand and your blade.

- Your wood may be worked without splintering or chipping if you use a blade that is sharp and a board that is flat.

6-Turn the saw off.

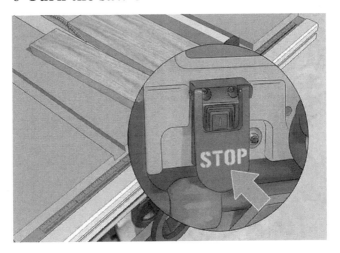

To turn off your table saw, just flip the switch located on the side of the machine. At this point, the board ought to be accurately cut to the measurements you had in mind.

Section 3-Creating A Crosscut

1-**First, adjust the blade so that it is appropriate for the thickness of the piece of wood that you are cutting**.

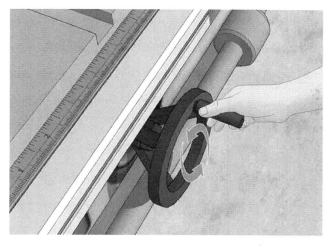

Set the height of the saw blade so that it is about 0.25 inches (0.635 cm) higher than the thickness of the board. If you put the blade at too high of an angle, it will shatter the wood, and if you set it at too low of an angle, it will not cut all the way through.

2-Position your miter gauge into its corresponding slot.

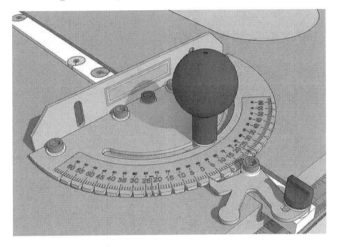

If your saw does not have a miter gauge built in, you will need to insert a separate gauge into the miter gauge slot, which is often located to the left of the saw blade. You can get a miter gauge at a hardware shop or buy one online if one wasn't included with your saw when you bought it.

3-Align the miter gauge with your blade using a square.

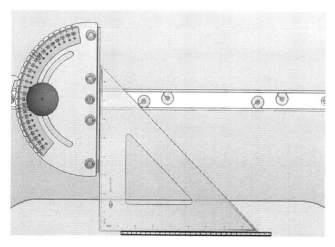

It is necessary to level the miter gauge with the sawblade in order to produce flawless crosscuts. Loosen the handle of the miter gauge, and then position a drafting triangle with a 45-degree angle along the length of your saw blade. Make the necessary adjustments to the gauge so that the blade and the miter gauge form a right angle with both of the sides of your drafting triangle. After it has been adjusted to perfection, retighten the handle on the gauge so that it remains in its current position.

4-Press your piece of lumber up to the fence of the miter gauge.

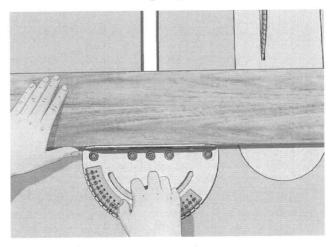

Pull the handle of the miter gauge with your right hand and position the gauge so that it is facing the rear of the saw. Put your left hand on the edge of the miter gauge, and firmly press the board you're holding against it. Maintain a distance of at least 15 centimeters (about 6 inches)

between your fingertips and the saw blade cover.

- On the miter gauge fence, the board should be positioned such that it is perpendicular to the blade at a 90-degree angle.

5-Try to push the board by means of through the blade.

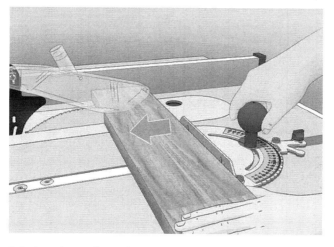

Maintain a firm hold on the board with your left hand as you push slowly but carefully with your right hand on the miter gauge handle. Cut your board by moving

the miter gauge fence forward and then
pushing it back.

**6-The board should be pulled back, and
the saw should be turned off.**

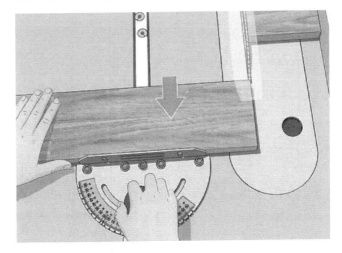

When you have finished cutting through
the piece of wood, bring the board back to
where it was before you started cutting.
You've just completed a crosscut by
turning off your table saw and doing so.

CHAPTER TWO

Instructional Guide To Cut Angles On Table Saw

A table saw is a versatile piece of equipment that can be used to cut wood in a variety of different ways. Even though cutting angles isn't the primary purpose of this tool, it is capable of doing it in a precise and accurate manner. In order to get a clean cut, preparation is essential. The cut has to be outlined on the wood first, and then the saw blade has to be adjusted to the suitable height. The saw should then be adjusted to the appropriate angle using a device such as a miter gauge. When you are ready to cut, ensure that you use the correct technique and take all necessary safety steps to avoid injuring yourself.

When everything is done properly, you will end up with cleanly cut wood that may elevate the quality of your project to the next level.

Items You Need

- Table saw
- Dust mask
- Pencil
- Drafting triangle or a similar tool
- Taper jig or Miter gauge
- Safety glasses
- Earplugs
- Scrap wood

Section 1-Make Sure The Wood And Saw Blade Are Adjusted Correctly

1-While you are working on prepping the wood, turn off the saw by unplugging it first.

During the course of your preparations, you will always move toward the saw's blade. Turn off the saw until you are ready to use it so that you do not cause any mishaps. It's acceptable to turn it off, but you should also unplug it fully from the electrical socket to make sure it can't be accidentally turned back on.

- When you are finished using the saw, be sure you always switch it off. This includes when you have completed the process of cutting the wood.

2-Make use of a ruler to determine the beginning and ending points of the cut you will be making.

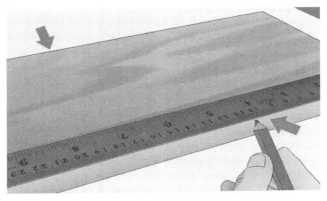

Determine the angle at which you want to cut the wood and mark it accordingly. In most cases, it entails figuring out the required dimensions of length and breadth for the job. Take measurements around the edges of the piece of wood while using a pencil to mark the locations. Check them again to make sure the angle is appropriate for the project you are working on.

● You may also use a measuring device such as a tape measure or similar measuring tool. Later on, when it is time to set the angle, you may use the same carpentry equipment, such as a drafting triangle or a framing square.

3-**Trace the outline of the cut with the pencil all the way across the board**.

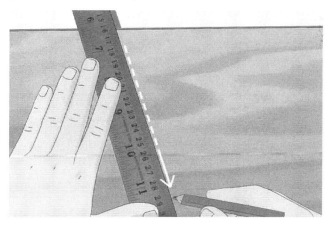

You should now connect the spots that you indicated to show where the cut will begin and terminate. Keep the ruler in place over the surface of the board as you draw a thick, black line across it. Make certain that the line is not only straight but also quite noticeable.

- Check that the outline you created is correct. You won't be able to make any more adjustments once you've begun cutting into the wood. Take another reading of the angle's measurement.

4-Adjust the saw's height so that it's approximately a quarter of an inch (0.64 cm).

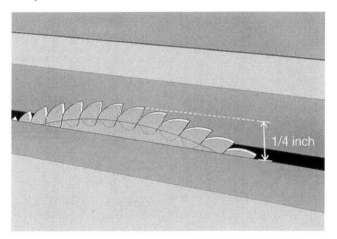

Table saws are equipped with an adjustment crank that allows the blade to be raised and lowered from its position inside the table. The correction may be made in a number of ways, one of which involves holding a ruler up to a piece of scrap wood. Put a mark at 0.64 centimeters (1/4 inch), then position it next to the saw. Raise the saw up until it is flush with the line.

- The standard setting for the blade is 1/8 inch (0.32 cm), which works well for making straight cuts but is less efficient for cutting at angles. When the height is increased, more of the blade's teeth are brought into contact with the wood, which results in a cut that is more precise and smooth.
- If you are unsure of the appropriate cutting height, lift the blade as high as you possibly can to make the cleanest cut possible.

Section 2-Placing The Wood In An
Angle Position

1-If you are going to be doing a cross cut, position a drafting triangle so that it is close to the saw.

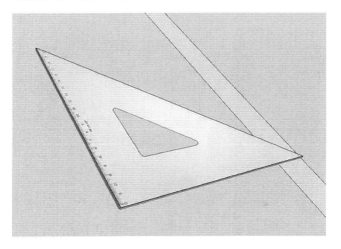

Combining the functions of a ruler and a ruler, the drafting triangle is an instrument used for accuracy and measurement. Due to the fact that it has flat edges, it is an excellent tool for preparing angled cuts. Before you use it, make sure that the table saw is clean of any other debris. Make sure you give yourself enough of space to select the angle at which you want to cut.

- A cross cut is a cut that is done either perpendicular to the grain of the wood or across the breadth of a board. Use a taper jig instead of a standard saw if you need to cut along the edges or along the length of the material.

- If you do not have access to a drafting triangle, you may use another instrument that has a flat edge, such as a framing square. A framing square is another combination measuring tool; however, it is somewhat longer and broader than a regular square, which may make it simpler to use.

2-Position a miter gauge so that it is flush with the edge of the drafting triangle that is flat.

A miter gauge is a convenient tool that holds boards at an angle as you cut them, allowing you to work more efficiently. It is in the shape of a half circle and has a number of marks on it that correlate to various angles. Keep the gauge pressed up against one of the flat sides of the triangle. Take note of the marks on the gauge, since they will be used to determine the angle at which the wood should be positioned.

- Two of the sides of a drafting triangle are flat, while the third edge is diagonal. When it comes to establishing an angle, it is often simpler to deal with the flat edges.

3-**To adjust the angle, move the gauge to the left or right as needed.**

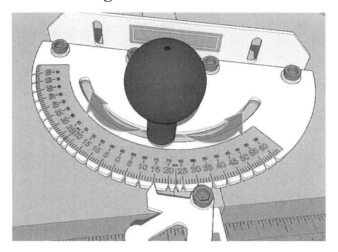

Maintain the pressed gauge made of wood and the drawing triangle in the same pressed position. The handle of the miter gauge will move in response to the movement of the triangle, causing it to point to one of the marks on the gauge's angle scale. After you have turned it so that the handle displays the appropriate angle for your project, spin the handle clockwise to secure it in place at that angle.

- It might be challenging to find the optimal angular position. Because miter gauges are sensitive, you will need to make little adjustments in both directions, one at a time, until you get it to the desired setting.

- If you want to cut an angle that is exactly 90 degrees, you should position the miter gauge so that it is against one end of the drawing triangle and the saw blade should be positioned against the other end. You don't even need to make modifications.

4-If you are going to be doing lengthy cuts or bevel cuts, you should use a taper jig.

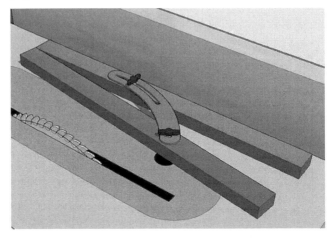

Long pieces of wood that are used to reinforce the side of a board are known as standard taper jigs. In order to keep your fingertips away from the blade when doing rip cuts and bevel cuts, it is used in place of a miter gauge. Place the jig so that it is resting against the side of the board that is opposite the cut. The fence of the saw will be able to rest against the reverse side of the jig.

- Rip cuts are cuts that are done along the length of the board, which is also parallel to the direction of the grain in the wood. Bevel cuts are cuts of an angled kind that are done along the board's edge.

- The taper jigs in the form of a triangle are relatively dated and difficult to use compared to other types. Obtaining a jig in the form of a sled will both simplify and improve the safety of the procedure. Because it comes with a base and clamps that can be adjusted to suit the wood, you won't have to hold onto the wood as it moves closer to the saw.

5-The wood has to be positioned at the appropriate angle, so open the taper jig.

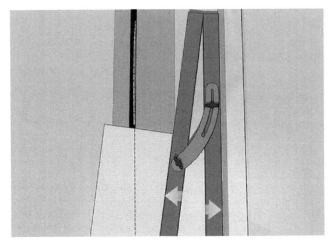

While you are working on this, make sure that the piece of wood is firmly placed on the jig's edge. To determine the distance from the jig to the ends of the cut you want to make, you may use a measuring tape. Check to see that the distance between both points and the jig is the same.

- In order to outline the cut, taper jigs might be used. After you have taken measurements and marked the endpoints, you may use a ruler to join them together. When using the saw, be sure to follow these operating instructions.

6-Put up a fence around the wood so you are able to control it.

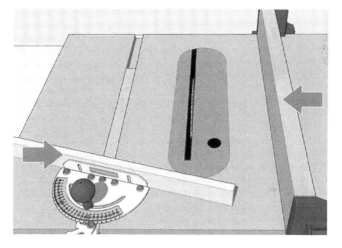

A fence is a metal bar that is attached to table saws and acts as a vital part of the saw's safety system. Move the fence so that it supports the miter gauge or taper jig as you slide it along the table. If you do not have a fence, you may substitute a piece of scrap wood by sliding it into the clamp that is located on the front of the miter jig or the rear of the taper jig. You are able to keep the piece of wood in place thanks to the fence, which also creates some distance between your fingers and the blade of the saw.

- If you were using a drafting triangle, you should put it away and start using the fence instead.

Section 3-Utilizing The Table Saw

1-Before using the table saw, ensure that you are properly outfitted in protective gear.

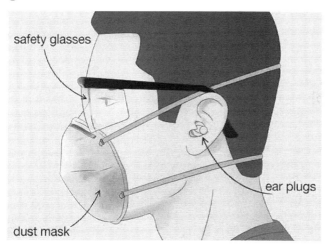

safety glasses

ear plugs

dust mask

When working with wood, it is imperative that you use protective eyewear, such as goggles or safety glasses. In addition, invest in a quality set of earplugs so that you can better cope with the saw's loudness. Wearing a dust mask will provide you with extra safety by preventing sawdust from getting into your lungs.

- Ensure that your working space has enough ventilation by opening any doors or windows that are nearby. If you have any ventilation fans, you should turn them on.

- It is important that you keep other people and animals away from the area until you have had the opportunity to clean up and turn off the table saw.

2-**Before moving on with your project, practice your cutting skills by making a few test cuts.**

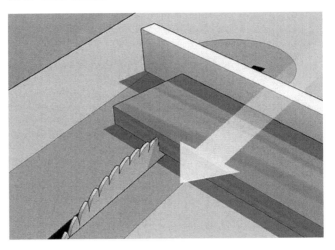

Make sure that your saw and miter gauge are in good working condition by using the test cuts. Pick out a few of pieces of scrap wood, and then cut those pieces in the same manner that you want to cut the wood for your project. Check that the saw leaves a clean cut through each of the pieces. Make modifications as required.

- If you are cutting an angle of 45 degrees, you will need to cut two separate pieces and then attempt to put them together. The boards that are cut in this manner should have an easy time joining together. If they don't, then the precision of your miter gauge's settings is off.

- You won't be able to put the boards through the same kind of test if they have been cut at an angle other than 45 degrees. Examine the cuts to ensure

that they have a smooth appearance.
After that, give your miter gauge a
second look to ensure that it is set the
way you want it to be.

**3-If you are going to do a bevel cut, this
phase require you to stand the board on
its end.**

Bevel cuts are made along the edges of the
board, which makes them somewhat more
challenging to execute accurately. Adjust
the saw so that it is perpendicular to the
guideline you just established. Check to

ensure that the wood is positioned flush against the fence. After that, use the saw in the same manner that you would if you were making a cross cut across the width of the board.

- When using a miter saw, making bevel cuts is a lot less difficult. If you have the ability to do so, choose a different set of tools.

- Your fingertips might come dangerously near to being cut by the saw. Put some force into the wood by prodding it with a stick.

4-Lean the piece of scrap wood hard against the fence while holding it firmly in one hand.

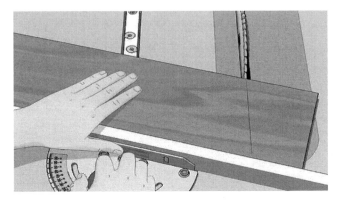

Put the fence in front of the hand that you use most often at the edge of the table. The wood is positioned between the fence and the saw at this point. Adjust the saw so that it is parallel to the cutting guideline that you drew. Before you start cutting, check that the miter gauge is not in the way of the saw by moving it out of the way.

● Grab the other end of the piece of wood and the fence rather than the side you want to cut. Keep a distance of at least

6 inches (15 cm) between your hand and the blade to reduce the risk of injury.

- In most situations, it does not make a difference which hand you use to grasp the wood in your hand. It is more crucial to have control over it, and having control over it is made simpler when you use your dominant hand.

5-Position yourself so that the saw blade is behind the piece of wood you are cutting.

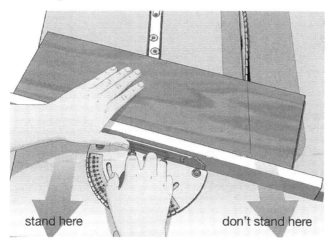

stand here   don't stand here

Make a couple of steps in the direction of your dominant hand as you go to the side. Instead of positioning yourself directly behind the saw blade, put yourself directly behind the miter gauge. You will be protected against a phenomenon known as backfire if you stand in this stance. Although it's not very common, it might occur even when you least expect it.

- The phenomenon known as "kickback" occurs when the piece of wood that you are chopping unexpectedly shoots back at your face. It's risky, but if you move to the side, you can avoid being struck by whatever is coming at you.

- In the event that the piece of wood transforms into a projectile, check to see that you are not hiding anything precious or hazardous behind you.

6-Put some pressure on the board, and move it closer to the saw blade.

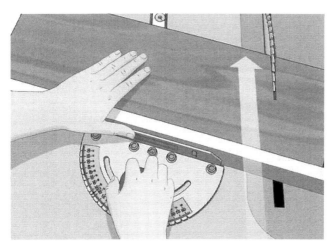

Put your non-dominant hand on the handle of the miter gauge as you continue to keep the board and fence together with your dominant hand. After that, you should have everything moving ahead at a pace that is constant and consistent. Move gently in order to get a consistent cut and to prevent backlash. When the saw has completely penetrated the wood, you should stop cutting.

- At first, getting the hang of the movement could be a little challenging. Keep in mind that going slower is preferable and safer. However, after the board reaches the saw, do not stop pushing it ahead in the forward direction.
- The fence will sustain some minor damage as a result of the saw. It won't make a difference as long as you use a piece of scrap wood or something equally disposable.
- Switch to using a wood stick whenever your hand will be in danger of getting too near to the saw, such as when cutting a board along its length. Make use of the stick to secure the board to the ground while you complete passing it over the blade.

7-After cutting through the wood, you should pull it back.

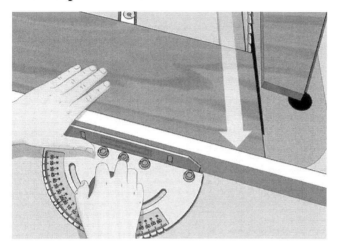

After the board has been completely sliced through by the saw, bring everything back toward you. The fence and the miter gauge are both included in this price. Bring it closer to the side of the table where it belongs. After turning off the saw, you may securely remove the piece of wood from the miter gauge and then remove it from your possession.

- Verify that the wood has been finished to your satisfaction before purchasing it. It need to have a clean edge, and it ought to be cut at the appropriate angle for your undertaking. It's possible that you'll need to redo the cutting if it doesn't seem just perfect.

Made in the USA
Middletown, DE
29 September 2023

39773400R00031